Elegant Lacé®

Gerda Perik

FORTE PUBLISHERS

Contents

ISBN 90 5877 375 2

This is a publication from
Forte Publishers BV
P.O. Box 1394
3500 BJ Utrecht
The Netherlands

For more information about the
creative books available from
Forte Publishers:
www.hobby-party.com

Publisher: Marianne Perlot
Editor: Hanny Vlaar
Photography and digital image
editing: Fotografie Gerhard Witteveen,
Apeldoorn, the Netherlands
Cover and inner design:
BADE creatieve communicatie, Baarn,
the Netherlands
Translation: TextCase, Groningen,
the Netherlands

Preface

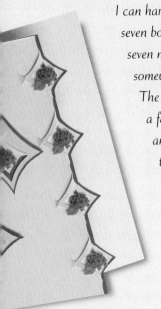

I can hardly believe it, but this is my eighth Lacé book. After the success of the first seven books, it was a challenge for me to create attractive, new designs with the seven new templates. I hope I have succeeded. The style of the new templates somewhat resembles that of my first two books. Again the points can be secured. The collection of Lacé templates has become so large now, that there will be a favourite template for everyone, from simple and elegant to complicated and with an intricate design. Two very small Lacé templates have been added too. They come in very handy for decorating cards or for making labels for presents, a bunch of flowers etc.

All of the examples can be made using the well-known shiny Lacé duo-colour card. However, I have used new duo-colour card in lots of bright colour combinations.

Be inspired by the pretty cutting sheets of Marianne Design, Shake-it, Picturel, Marjoleine and Marij Rahder and put your craft gear ready.

Enjoy your cutting and folding *Gerda*

Thanks: Marianne for the much-appreciated support. Dini, my "cutting lady", for the many pleasant hours she spends with me, cutting the pictures.

Techniques

Lacé cutting

The pattern to be cut out is shown on the light green Lacé templates. Preferably use the attractive Lacé duo-colour card in the new, bright colours. Stick the template in the correct place on the card (not on the cutting mat) using non-permanent adhesive tape or Lacé tape.
I have also used the outside of the templates. Use the Lacé knife or an Olfa knife to cut through the openings, starting at the point and cutting towards the side. Hold the knife vertical when cutting. If you hold the knife like a pen, you will not be able to get right into the corners. Always use a knife with a sharp point. After cutting, carefully remove the template from the card. It is important that you first score the edges which are going to be folded using the Lacé scoring and folding tool. Fold the scored sections towards you and fold them under the grooves that you have not folded or into the triangles that you have cut especially for this purpose. You will now see the other side of the card. The colours on both sides compliment each other.

Left or right-handed people

It is easier for right-handed people to cut the template with the word Lacé at the top. For left- handed people, it is easier if the word Lacé is at the bottom.

Tip

For the templates with circular grooves, it is best if you rotate the card without removing the knife from the circular groove. If you remove the knife from the groove and then put it back again, there is a chance that you will not put the knife back on exactly the same spot. This will result in an uneven edge on the card.

Eyelets

Eyelets come in various designations and various shapes and sizes, but basically they are no more than a metal ring with a round hole and a tip at the bottom that must be flattened to secure the ring. (Certain eyelets are a two-component system where you need two rings: a large one and a somewhat smaller one. You hammer them together using special "tools". They are mainly intended for use in clothing.) You can get eyelets in any colour or shape: circles, flowers, hearts, leaves etc. You can also use round eyelets in combination with a flat shape e.g. a flower, a hand, a Christmas tree or even a cake and candles. Look around in the craft shop and you will see that there are lots of possible variations and combinations.

1. The new Lacé templates.

2. Cut the pattern, score/fold the corners and insert the points in the little incisions.

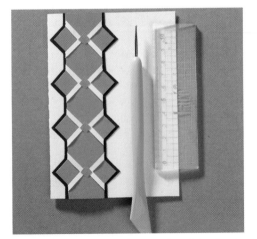

3. The scoring and folding tool and the Lacé ruler.

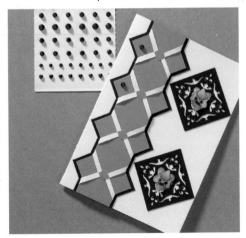

4. Finish the card with 3D pictures and decorative stones

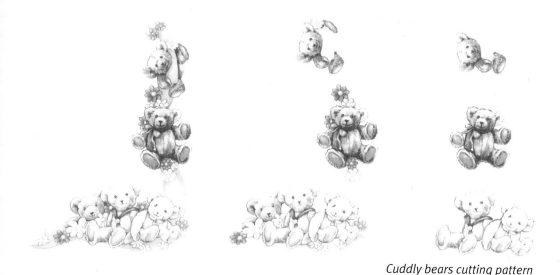

Cuddly bears cutting pattern

You need a toolkit to apply the eyelets.
Instructions: punch a hole in the card with the striking tool (you may also use the Fiskars hand punch with the 1/8" circle) using a hammer and a soft old cutting mat. Push an eyelet or a flower (or another shape) with an eyelet into the hole. Turn the card over and carefully hit the tip open at the back using the hammer and the striking tool.
If you put two eyelets in the card, not too far apart, you can thread a ribbon, cord or string through them. This makes them very handy for hanging labels etc.

3D cutting

Cutting instructions are included for most of the pictures. For very small pictures, only stick one layer on the card using a bead of 3D glue or some foam tape.
First puff up the pictures using a shaping pen or your fingers.
Carry out the following if you use other pictures: cut the entire picture out first. Look what is in the background and do not cut that out for the second layer.
Finally, for the third layer, only cut out what is in the foreground.

Materials

- Card: Artoz (A),
  Canson Mi-Teintes (C) and
  Papicolor (P)
- Duo-colour card in bright
  colours
- Lacé duo-colour card in
  various colours
- Lacé templates 49 to 53b
- Lacé knife or Olfa knife
- Lacé ruler

- Lacé scoring and folding tool
- Lacé cutting mat
- Eyelets and shapes in
  various colours
- Eyelets toolkit (punch and
  striking tool)
- Figure punches
- Border ornament punches
- Hand punches (Fiskars)
- Corner punches

- Corner ornament punches
- Cutting sheets: Marianne
  Design, Shake-it, Picturel,
  Marjoleine and Marij Radher
- Border stickers, decorative
  stickers and text stickers
- Identi-pens
- Cutting mat, knife
- Transparent ruler with metal
  cutting edge (Securit)

Cuddly bears cutting pattern

Colourful combinations

Pink with two shades of blue is a nice colour combination.

1. Card with two labels

Card: dark blue (A417), snowy white (P30) and blue/pink duo-colour card 432 o cutting sheet Picturel 541 • ribbons • corner ornament punch 2726 • Fiskars hand punch 2560 • eyelets • line stickers • Lacé template 52b

Make a double card of 13.5 x 13.5 cm from duo-colour card. Make three squares: white - 13 x 13 cm, dark blue - 0.5 cm smaller and duo-colour card again 0.5 cm smaller. Cut two rectangles of 9 cm high and 4.3 wide from the pink square at 1.5 cm from the edges. Punch out the corners. Make two blue labels by cutting around the circumference of the template, stick them on white card and cut the card with a 2 mm wider border. Punch eyelets in the labels and the pink card. Use ribbons to hang the labels over the "window". Decorate the card with punched out hearts and a sticker border. Secure the pictures with 3D glue.

2. A label

Card: dark blue (A417) and blue/pink duo-colour card 432 • cutting sheet Marij Rahder 2316 • eyelets gold • Lacé templates: 50 and 52b

Make a double card of 14.8 x 10.5 cm from duo-colour card (fold on the left). Make a dark blue strip of 14.8 x 4.5 cm and a strip of duo-colour card which is 0.5 cm smaller again. Cut the pattern in the duo-colour card; do not cut the central grooves. Make a label from a scrap piece of duo-colour card and cut it around the circumference of the template. Stick it on dark blue card and cut this with a 2 mm wide border. Punch eyelets in the label and the pattern and tie the label to the card with a ribbon. Stick two pictures on dark blue card of 3.2 x 3.2 cm and make the picture 3D.

3. Blackberry blossom

Card: dark blue (A417), blue/pink duo-colour card 432 and snowy white (P30) • white sticker border • cutting sheet Marij Rahder 2316 • Lacé template 53a

Make a double card of 14.8 x 10 cm from duo-colour card and a dark blue strip of 14.8 x 8 cm. Cut the pattern in duo-colour card of 14.8 x 5.8 cm and cut the card by cutting around the circumference of the template. Stick the strip on white card and cut this with a 2 mm wide

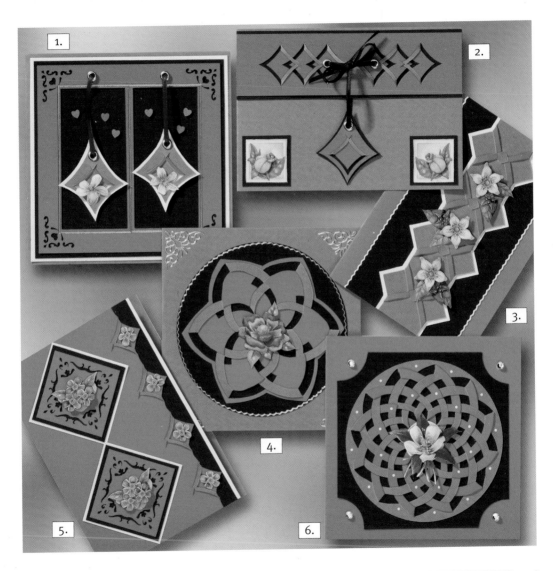

border. Decorate the card with white sticker borders and 3D pictures.

4. Blue/pink cut flower

Card: dark blue (A417) and blue/pink duo-colour card 432 • stickers: corners and lines • cutting sheet Marij Rahder 2317 • Lacé template 49

Make a double card of 13 x 13 cm from duo-colour card. Also make a dark blue circle (Ø 11 cm) and a circle (Ø 11.5 cm) from duo-colour card. Cut the flower pattern in the duo-colour card circle; cut every third line (every other pattern). Cut the outer border of the "flower" 2 mm wide. Decorate the card with sticker corners and borders. Stick a 3D picture in the centre.

5. Collage card

Card: dark blue (A417), snowy white (P30) and blue/pink duo-colour card 432 • cutting sheet Marij Rahder 2317 • corner ornament punch 2730 • Lacé template 52a

Make a double card of 14.8 x 10.5 cm from duo-

colour card. Cut the pattern out of the right-hand side of the card, 2 cm from the edge. Cut the card around the circumference of the template. Glue dark blue card of 14.8 x 9.5 cm on the inside of the card on the left-hand side, and then white card of 14.8 x 10 cm. Cut three times two squares: white - 5.2 x 5.2 cm, dark blue - 4.9 x 4.9 cm and duo-colour card - 4.5 x 4.5 cm. Punch out the corners of the smallest square. Stick 3D flowers on the squares and secure the flowers along the border using 3D glue.

6. Cut circular flower

Card: dark blue (A417) and blue/pink duo-colour card 432 • decorative stones blank • white sticker dots • cutting sheet Picturel 540 • double photo corner punch 2634 • Lacé template 49

Make a double card of 13 x 13 cm from duo-colour card. Also make a dark blue square of 11.5 x 11.5 cm. Punch out its corners. Make a circle (Ø 10.5 cm) from duo-colour card. Cut the whole pattern in this circle. Decorate the card with sticker dots, decorative stones and a 3D picture.

Springtime

Cards in merry

spring colours.

1. Pick-me-up
Card: dark green (A309) and yellow/green duo-colour card 433 • decorative stones • cutting sheet Picturel 542 • text sticker • Lacé template 51
Make a double card of 14.8 x 10.5 cm from duo-colour card. Fold the card open and cut half a circle (Ø 7 cm) in the right-hand side of the front card. Then fold the front card in half (see photograph). Cut diagonal Lacé patterns in the corners at the bottom and the top. Stick a dark green circle (Ø 7 cm) on it. Decorate the card with decorative stones and a 3D picture.

2. Ducklings
Card: dark green (A309) and green/yellow duo-colour card 433 • figure punch 7003 • cutting sheet Marij Rahder 2325 • stickers • Lacé template 53a
Make a double card of 15 x 10.5 cm from duo-colour card. Cut the pattern in duo-colour card of 15 x 5.8 cm. Cut the card around the circumference of the template. Stick the strip that you have cut on dark green card and cut this with a 2 mm wide border. Cut four squares: two yellow ones of 4.2 x 4.2 cm and two dark green ones of 4 x 4 cm. Punch out the corners of the dark green squares. Stick it all on the card and finish the card with stickers. Make the picture 3D.

3. Rabbit plays hide and seek
Card: dark green (A309) and yellow/green duo-colour card 433 • cutting sheet Marij Rahder 2325 • Lacé template 50
Make a double card of 15 x 10.5 cm from duo-colour card. Cut the Lacé pattern diagonally in every corner. Stick dark green card on the

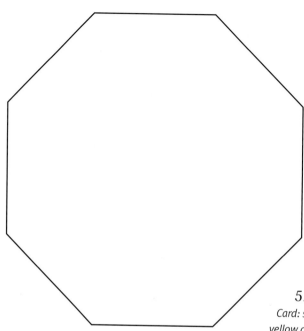

(see photograph). Cut a pattern in the bottom and top corners. Also cut a border pattern in the right-hand part of the card, at 1 cm from the edge. Cut the card around the circumference of the template. Stick a 15 x 10.5 cm dark green card behind it. Stick the picture on an 8.7 x 5.3 cm dark green rectangle. Decorate the card with decorative stones and make the picture 3D.

5. Duck family

Card: scrap piece of dark green (A309) and green/ yellow duo-colour card 433 • cutting sheet Marij Rahder 2318 • decorative stones • Lacé template 53a
Make a double card of 19 x 10.5 cm from duo-colour card. Cut an octagon out of the centre of the card (see illustration). Stick a dark green 2 mm wide frame around this. Stick the picture on a dark green octagon. Cut the pattern in a scrap piece of yellow/green duo-colour card and cut around the circumference of the template. Stick the strips on dark green card and cut this with a slightly wider border. Stick all layers on the card and make the picture 3D. Stick decorative stones in the pattern.

inside on the left-hand side. Stick the picture on a dark green circle (Ø 8 cm) and make it 3D.

4. Butterflies

Card: dark green (A309) and yellow/green duo-colour card 433 • cutting sheet Marij Rahder 2316 • gold decorative stones • Lacé template 53a
Make a double card of 15 x 10.5 cm from duo-colour card. Fold the card open and cut a 3 cm wide and 9 cm high rectangle in the right-hand side of the front card. Then fold the card in half

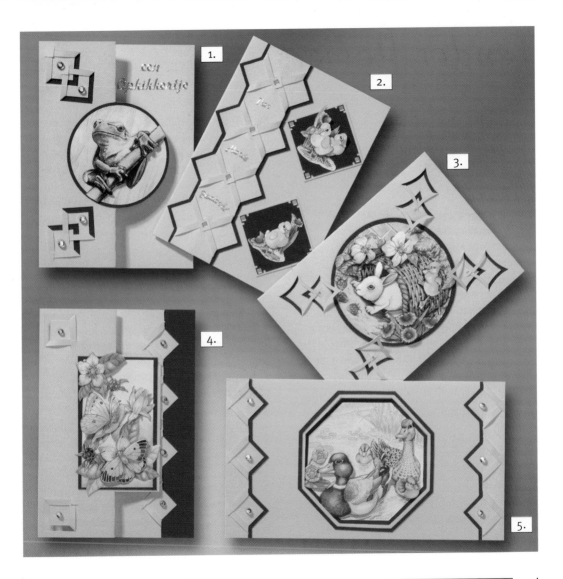

Tender flowers

Forget-me-nots for special greeting cards.

1. The pink circle

Card: dark blue (A417), cornflower (A425) and pink/white duo-colour card 434 • cutting sheet Shake-it IT 404 • sticker borders • mini split pin • sticker dots • Lacé template 49

Make a double dark blue card of 13 x 13 cm. Cut two circles: cornflower blue (Ø 12 cm) and duo-colour card (Ø 11 cm). Cut the pattern in the latter one; Stick everything on the card. The label has been secured to the card with a mini split pin in the centre of the pattern. Decorate the card with stickers. The pictures are attached to the card using 3D glue.

2. Blue forget-me-nots

Card: snowy white (P30), lilac (P14) and blue/white duo-colour paper 436 • cutting sheet Shake-it IT 391 • sticker dots • Lacé template 53a

Make a double white card of 14.8 x 10.5 cm and a duo-colour card strip of 13.8 x 10 cm. Cut a pattern on the left- and right-hand sides of the latter. Cut the card around the circumference of the template, stick it on pink card and cut this with a 2 mm wider border. The flowers are secured in the pattern using 3D glue. Make a 3D bouquet in the centre.

3. Mini forget-me-nots

Card: snowy white (P30), lilac (P14) and blue/white duo-colour paper 436 • cutting sheet Shake-it IT 391 • border ornament punch 2336 • Lacé template 52a

Make a double white card of 14.8 x 10.5 cm. Punch out the borders of a pink strip of 14 x 9.5 cm. Cut the pattern in a scrap piece of duo-colour card of 13.7 x 6 cm. Cut the card around the circumference of the template. Stick three white circles (Ø 2.7 cm) in the pattern. Decorate the card with sticker dots and flowers which you secure to the card with 3D glue.

4. Flying butterflies

Card: snowy white (P30), lilac (P14), dark blue (A417) and blue/white duo-colour card 436 • Shake-it cutting sheets: IT 389 and IT 391 • Lacé template 49

Make a double white card of 13 x 13 cm, a pink square of 12.5 x 12.5 cm and a dark blue square of 12 x 12 cm. Cut the "flower" in duo-colour card; cut every third line. Cut out the border of the "flower" 0.5 cm wide. Stick a 2.5 cm pink circle in the centre. Decorate the card with butterflies and flowers which you secure with 3D glue.

5. Pink strip with flowers

Card: cornflower (A425), snowy white (P30), dark blue (A417) and pink/white duo-colour card 434
• sticker borders and corners • cutting sheet Shake-it IT 404 • Lacé template 53a
Make a double cornflower blue card of 15 x 10.5 cm. Stick a white rectangle of 14.3 x 9.5 cm on this. Cut the pattern in a strip of duo-colour card of 14.3 x 5.5 cm. Cut the card around the circumference of the template, stick it on dark blue card and cut this with a 2 mm wider border. Decorate the card with stickers and apply the flowers with 3D glue.

6. Only flowers

Card: dark blue (A417), cornflower (A425) and pink/white duo-colour card 434 • cutting sheet Shake-it IT 404 • pink pen • Lacé template 49
Make a double dark blue card of 14 x 14 cm. Then cut a cornflower blue square of 13.5 x 13.5 cm and cut a 2 mm smaller square from duo-colour card. Cut the flower pattern in the smaller square; cut every third line. Secure the pictures in the corners. Cut out the flowers again and secure them with 3D glue. Draw pink lines along the ruler.

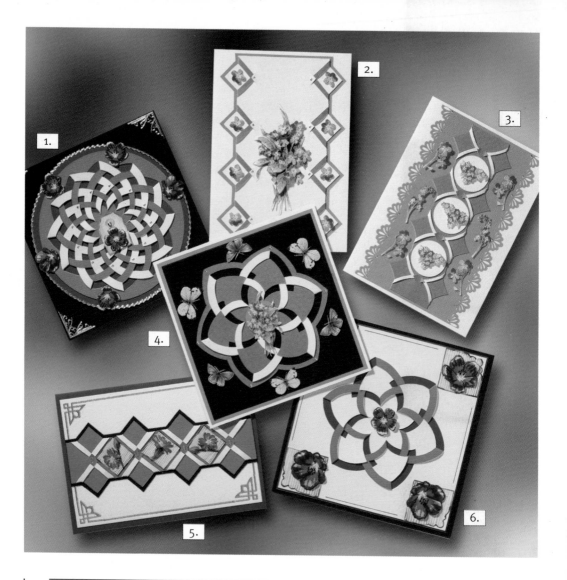

Label cards

Why not decorate your cards with labels and little flowers?

1. Blue label card

Card: snowy white (P30), rust-coloured (C504) and blue/white duo-colour card 436 • eyelets blue • rust-coloured ribbon • cutting sheet Shake-it IT 401 • Lacé template 52a

Make a double white card of 15 x 10.5 cm (fold at the top) and a rust-coloured card of 14.5 x 10 cm. Cut the pattern in duo-colour card of 14 x 9.5 cm. Stick the pictures of the labels first on dark blue card and then on rust-coloured card. Cut every consecutive layer 2 mm larger. The rust-coloured square in the centre is 3.5 x 3.5 cm. Stick on the picture and make it 3D. Punch eyelets in the labels and the card as shown in the example. Use ribbons to hang the labels from the pattern. Decorate the card with 3D pictures.

2. Two little pink labels

Card: snowy white (P30), dark blue (A417) and pink/white duo-colour card 434 • cutting sheet Shake-it IT 402 • blue ribbon • mini split pins • Lacé templates: 51 and 53b

Make a double white card of 15 x 10.5 cm with the fold at the top. Also make a dark blue card of 14.5 x 10 cm and a duo-colour card of 14 x 9.5 cm. Cut the pattern in the duo-colour card. Score and fold the lines you have cut and thread a ribbon through them. Also make two labels from duo-colour card and secure them to the card using split pins. Stick a dark blue square of 2.4 x 2.4 cm between the pattern using 3D glue. Decorate the card with 3D pictures.

3. Cut pink flower

Card: snowy white (P30), dark blue (A417) and pink/white duo-colour card 434 • sticker border and text • cutting sheet Shake-it IT 402 • Lacé template 49

Make a double white card of 13 x 13 cm. Cut the "flower" pattern in the duo-colour card by cutting every third line. Cut the outer border of the "flower" 0.5 cm wide. Stick the duo-colour card on dark blue card and cut this with a 0.5 mm wide border. Apply a sticker border and stick the little flowers and leaves on the card using 3D glue.

4. Pink labels in the centre of the card

Card: snowy white (P30), dark blue (A417) and pink/white duo-colour card 434 • cutting sheet Shake-it IT 402 • Lacé template 52b

Make a double white card of 13 x 13 cm and a dark blue square of 12 x 12 cm.. Make four labels from duo-colour card. Cut them around the circumference of the template. Then stick them in the centre of the card. Cut a white circle (Ø 2.2 cm) and stick it in the centre between the labels. Decorate the card with 3D pictures which you secure with 3D glue.

5. Cute white/blue labels

Card: snowy white (P30), rust-coloured (C504) and blue/white duo-colour card 436 • cutting sheet Shake-it IT 401 • corner ornament punch 2731 • sticker borders and text • Lacé template 53b

Make a double white card of 13 x 13 cm. Punch out the corners of a square of 12 x 12 cm made of duo-colour card. Make four labels from duo-colour card and stick them on a rust-coloured circle (Ø 10 cm). Make a 2 x 2 cm square from duo-colour card and stick it in the centre between the labels. Apply sticker borders and dots. Secure the flowers with 3D glue.

Summer cards

Fresh colours for all festive moments.

1. Label card

Card: white (P30), a scrap piece of purple (P46) and yellow/white duo-colour card 435 • eyelets yellow • purple ribbon • cutting sheet Lacé • Lacé templates: 52a and 52b

Make a double card of 14.8 x 10.5 cm from duo-colour card. Also make two labels from duo-colour card and cut them around the circumference of the template. Stick them on purple card and cut this with a 2 mm wide border. Punch a hole in each of the labels. Then punch eyelets in the white card as shown in the example and hang the labels on a ribbon. Secure the ribbons with adhesive tape on the rear. Cut the pattern at 2 cm from the right hand side of the card and cut the card around the circumference of the template. Stick a purple card on the inside on the left-hand side and cut it off at 2 mm from the pattern. Decorate the card with little flowers which you secure to the card with 3D glue.

2. Congratulations

Card: white (A211), purple (P46) and yellow/white duo-colour card 435 • cutting sheet Picturel 541 • Fiskars hand punch circular 1/8" • Identi-pen purple • purple ribbon • text sticker • Lacé template 51

Make a double white card of 14.8 x 10.5 cm. Also make two rectangles: purple of 14.5 x 10.2 cm and duo-colour card of 14.3 x 10 cm. Cut the pattern on the left-hand side in the yellow triangle. Punch a hole in the two central patterns and thread and tie a purple ribbon through them. Use an Identi-pen to colour the sticker circles purple while they are still on the sticker sheet. (You can also colour the text sticker this way.) Decorate the card with a text and a 3D picture.

3. Get Well Soon

Card: white (P30), purple (P46) and pink/white duo colour card 434 • cutting sheet Picturel 540 • decorative stones pink • text sticker • Lacé template 52a

Make a double white card of 14.8 x 10.5 cm. Cut a 13.5 x 6 cm strip from duo-colour card and cut the pattern. Cut the card along the border. Stick the strip that you have cut on purple card and cut this with a slightly wider border. Decorate the card with decorative stones, a text sticker and a 3D picture.

4. Let flowers speak for you

Card: snowy white (P30), purple (P46) and pink/white duo-colour card 434 • cutting sheet Picturel 543 • decorative stones gold • border and text stickers • Lacé template 53a

Make a double white card of 13 x 13 cm. Make two squares: purple of 12.5 x 12.5 cm and duo-colour card of 12 x 12 cm. Cut the pattern in the centre of the smaller square. Keep rotating the template by quarter turns. Make a square border around the pattern using stickers. Decorate the card with decorative stones, a text sticker and a 3D picture.

5. Sending a card just because you feel like it

Card: snowy white (P30), purple (P46) and yellow/white duo-colour card 435 • cutting sheet Marij Rahder 2319 • Identi-pen purple • sticker circles • corner ornament punch 2730 • Lacé template 49

Make a double white card of 13.5 x 13.5 cm. Make two squares: purple of 12.5 x 12.5 cm and duo-colour card of 12 x 12 cm. Punch out the corners of the smaller square and cut the pattern in its centre by cutting every third line. Use an Identi-pen to colour the sticker circles purple while they are still on the sticker sheet. (You can also colour the text sticker this way.) Decorate the card with little flowers which you secure with 3D glue.

Cuddly bears

A chapter especially for my granddaughter who loves her cuddly toys so much.

1. Lots of cuddly toys

Card: white (A211), aquamarine (A363) and dark blue/green duo-colour card 431 • cutting sheet Picturel 545 • decorative stones • Lacé template 53a

Make a double white card of 15 x 10.5 cm. Cut the pattern on the left in a strip of duo-colour card of 13.7 x 9.5 cm. Cut the card around the circumference of the template, then stick it on aquamarine card which you cut just a little larger. Decorate the card with decorative stones and lots of little cuddly toys in 3D.

2. Hugs and kisses

Card: white (A211), aquamarine (A363) and dark blue/green duo-colour card 431 • cutting sheet Picturel 545 • decorative stones • Lacé template 53b

Make a double white card of 13 x 13 cm. Cut the Lacé label pattern 4x in duo-colour card. Cut the labels around the circumference of the template. Stick them on aquamarine card as shown in the example and cut this with a 2 mm wide border. Decorate the card with decorative stones, a text sticker and 3D pictures of cuddly toys.

3. Collage card with bears

Card: white (A211), pink graduated paper and dark blue/green duo-colour card 431 • cutting sheet Marjoleine • transparent stickers, squares and text • Lacé template 53a

Make a double white card of 14.8 x 10.5 cm. Cut the pattern in a strip of duo-colour card of 14.8 x 6 cm. Cut the card around the circumference of the template. Then stick the strip on pink

graduated paper and cut this with a 2 mm wide border. Cut out two pictures and stick a transparent sticker over them.
Then stick the pictures on the card and make the cuddly toys 3D.

4. Flower bears

Card: white (A211), pink graduated paper and dark blue/green duo-colour card 431 • cutting sheet Marjoleine • sticker corners • gold-colour pen • Lacé template 49

Make a double white card of 13 x 13 cm. Cut the "flower" pattern in duo-colour card. Cut every third line. Cut the edge of the pattern 0.5 cm wide. Cut a circle (Ø 11.5 cm) from pink graduated paper. This will be the substrate for the "flower". Decorate the card with stickers. Stick the bears on the "flower" using 3D glue.

5. A red rose for grumpy old daddy bear

Card: white (A211), aquamarine (A363) and dark blue/green duo-colour card 431 • sticker borders and corners • cutting sheet Picturel 545 • Lacé template 53b

Make a double white card of 13 x 13 cm. Now make an aquamarine circle (Ø 8 cm) and stick the 3D picture on it. Now make four Lacé labels

from duo-colour card and slide these around the aquamarine circle. Stick this all on the card using some foam tape. Decorate the card with sticker corners and borders. Make the picture

6. The bear in the hat

Card: white (A211), pink graduated paper and dark blue/green duo-colour card 431 • decorative stones pink • eyelets pink • old rose ribbon • cutting sheet Picturel 545 • Lacé templates: 52a and 52b

Make a double white card of 14.8 x 10.5 cm. Cut the pattern along the left- and right-hand edges of a strip of duo-colour card of 14.8 x 10 cm. Cut the card around the circumference of the template and stick it on pink graduated paper. Cut this paper a bit larger. Cut the pattern in a duo-colour card label. Punch an eyelet in the label and hang it from the blue strip using a ribbon. Then stick everything on the card. Make the bear 3D.

1.

DIKKE
KNUFFEL

2.

3.

4.

5.

6.

Only flowers

Merry cards in fresh and
bright colours.

1. Yellow/white cut flower (cover)

*Card: dark blue (A417), snowy white (P30), royal
blue (A427) and yellow/white duo-colour card 435
• cutting sheet Shake-it IT 403 • corner ornament
punch 2729 • text sticker • Lacé template 49*
Make a double dark blue card of 13 x 13 cm.
Make two squares: white of 12.2 x 12.2 cm and
royal blue 2 mm smaller. Punch out the corners
of the smallest square. Cut the "flower" in a
scrap piece of yellow/white duo-colour card by
cutting every other line of the pattern. Score
and fold the lines that you have cut and fold
them under the non-folded sections. Cut the
"flower" with an outer border of 0.5 cm. Stick
the various layers on the card and decorate the
card with 3D pictures. Secure them with 3D glue.

2. Yellow marsh-marigolds

*Card: snowy white (P30), dark green (A309) and
yellow/white duo-colour card 435 • cutting sheet
Shake-it IT 392 • text sticker and sticker dots
• Lacé template 52a*
Make a double white card of 14.8 x 10.5 cm and

a dark green strip of 14.2 x 10 cm. Also cut a
yellow/white duo-colour card of 13.8 x 9.5 cm.
Cut a border pattern in this on the left-hand side.
Cut one pattern in the bottom and top corners
on the right. Stick the layers on the card and
apply little flowers along the borders using 3D
glue. Make a 3D bouquet of flowers in the centre.

3. Flowers in squares

*Card: dark blue (A417), snowy white (P30), cornflower
(A425) and yellow/white duo-colour card 435 • cutting
sheet Shake-it IT 403 • corner ornament punch • sticker
borders and circles • Lacé template 52a*
Make a double dark blue card of 15 x 10.5 cm.
Punch out the corners of a single white card

of 14.3 x 9.5 cm. Cut the pattern in yellow/white duo-colour card of 14.3 x 5.5 cm and cut the card around the circumference of the template. Score and fold the lines that you have cut and fold them under the little points. Stick the strip that you have cut on royal blue card of 14.3 x 5 cm. Stick all layers on the card and apply some flowers using 3D glue. Decorate the card with stickers.

4. Yellow/white cut circle

Card: snowy white (P30), dark green (A309) and yellow/white duo-colour card 435 • cutting sheet Shake-it IT 392 • sticker border • Lacé template 49
Make a double white card of 13 x 13 cm and a green square of 12 x 12 cm. Cut the Lacé pattern in a yellow/white circle (Ø 11 cm) of duo-colour card. Score the lines and fold the edges and insert the points under the non-folded lines. Stick everything on the card and decorate the card with sticker dots, borders and 3D pictures.

5. Only labels

Card: dark blue (A417), cornflower (A425) and yellow/white duo-colour card 435 • eyelets: flowers and circles • gold ribbon • cutting sheet Shake-it IT 403 • double photo corner punch 2634 • Lacé templates: 52a and 52b
Make a double dark blue card of 19 x 10.5 cm

and a cornflower blue strip of 18.5 x 10 cm. Cut the pattern in yellow/white duo-colour card of 18 x 9.5 cm. Score the lines and fold them. Punch an eyelet in the centre of the pattern. Cut labels from scrap pieces of duo-colour card using Lacé template 52b. Punch eyelets in them too. Thread a ribbon through both eyelets and secure the ribbon on the rear of the yellow/white card using adhesive tape. Punch out the corners of the yellow/white card. Punch flower-shaped eyelets in the corners of the cornflower blue card. Secure the labels with 3D glue if necessary and apply little flowers.

6. A bunch of daisies

Card: snowy white (P30), dark green (A309) and yellow/white duo-colour card 435 • cutting sheet Shake-it IT 390 • sticker border • Lacé template 52a
Make a double white card of 14.8 x 10.5 cm and a dark green strip of 14 x 10 cm. Cut the pattern in yellow/white duo-colour card of 13 x 9 cm, at the bottom and the top. Score the lines and fold them under the little incisions. Finish the card with 3D daisies and sticker borders

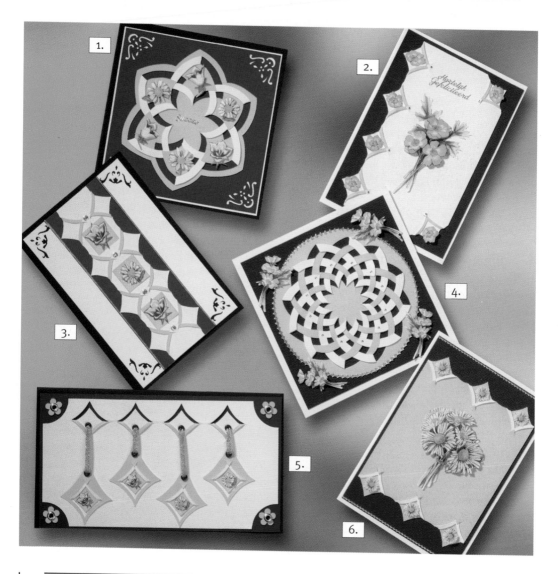

Dogs

You will please lots of people with this card, because 'dog is a man's best friend'.

1. Puppy with ball

Card: red (A517), white (A211), cornflower (A425) and yellow/white duo-colour card 435 • border ornament punch 2338 • cutting sheet Picturel 547 • decorative stones • Lacé template 53a

Make a double red card of 15 x 10.5 cm and two white strips of 15 x 9.5 cm and cornflower blue of 15 x 9.5 cm. Punch out the borders of the cornflower blue strip. Cut the pattern in yellow/white duo-colour card of 15 x 7 cm. Score and fold the lines and insert them behind the corners cut. Stick the layers on the card. Apply a 3D dog and decorative stones.

2. Puppies play with a log

Card: cornflower (A425), red (A517) and yellow/white duo-colour card 435 • cutting sheet Picturel 547 • decorative stones • Lacé template 50

Make a double cornflower card of 11.5 x 14 cm (with the fold on the left) and a red strip of 12.7 x 10.5 cm. Cut the pattern in the corners of yellow/white duo-colour card of 12.2 x 9.8 cm. Apply the picture and cut the little corners for inserting the Lacé pattern through the picture. Make the picture 3D and apply decorative stones.

3. Max with the latest news

Card: red (A517) and yellow/white duo-colour card 435 • cutting sheet Picturel 547 • buttons cutting sheet Eline AK 0029 • red ribbon • Lacé templates 53a and 53b

Make a double card of 15 x 10.5 cm from yellow/white duo-colour card. Cut the pattern in yellow/

white duo-colour card of 14.5 x 4 cm and cut the card around the circumference of the template. Do the same with the two small labels. Stick the strip that you have cut and the hangers on red card and cut this with a 2 mm wide border all round. Stick everything on the card and secure the labels with a red ribbon. Decorate the card with little flower buttons and a 3D picture.

4. Dogs and their toys

Card: red (A517), royal blue (A427) and yellow/white duo-colour card 435 • cutting sheet Picturel 547 • sticker dots • decorative stones • red ribbon • Fiskars hand punch circular 1/8" • Lacé templates: 50 and 52b

Make a double red card of 13.5 x 13.5 cm and a blue square of 12.5 x 12.5 cm. Cut the pattern in two places in yellow/white duo-colour card of 12 x 12 cm. Score the lines and fold them. Cut a label using Lacé template 52b. Stick it on a scrap piece of red card and cut this with a 2 mm wider border. Hang the label from the upper pattern by a red ribbon. Decorate the card with sticker dots, decorative stones and a 3D picture.

5. Little rascal and butterfly

Card: cornflower (A425), a scrap piece of red (A517)
and yellow/white duo-colour paper 435 • cutting sheet
Picturel 547 • flower button cutting sheet Eline AK
0029 • white ribbon • Fiskars hand punch circular 1/8"
• Lacé template 50

Make a double cornflower blue card of 14.8 x
10.5 cm. Cut the pattern in yellow/white duo-
colour card of 14 x 10 cm. Stick the picture on a
red circle (Ø 8 cm). Punch out two holes and
attach the circle with a ribbon. Stick the layers on
the card.

Use a needle and thread to stitch on the flower
buttons of the cutting sheet in the corners, as if
they were real buttons. Make the picture 3D.

Many thanks to Kars & Co B.V. in Ochten, the Netherlands for providing the material.
Shopkeepers can order the materials from Kars & Co B.V. in Ochten, the Netherlands.